And You Call Yourself a Christian

By Darick "DDS" Spears

And You Call Yourself a

Christian

Written and "UN-Edited"

by Darick "DDS" Spears

Rated : "SO REAL"

© 2017 DDS MediaWorks LLC
The 21st Century Shakespears
Publishing

And You Call Yourself A Christian
Copyright © 2017 by Darick Spears

All rights reserved. No part of this book may be reproduced or transmitted in any form or by any means without written permission from the author.

**ISBN-13: 978-0692992456
(The 21st Century Shakespears
Publishing)**

**ISBN-10:
0692992456**

**Printed in USA by DDS MediaWorks LLC./21st
Century Shakespears Publishing**

And You Call Yourself a Christian by Darick Spears

Disclaimer: Break Every Chain

Before you enter into this book, I want you to do one thing. That is break off the chains on your brain and be open-minded. I have lived everything that you are about to read about. And I feel it's my responsibility to give back to those people who have not yet received Christ in their lives, and for the ones who have already received and taken on the journey.

Being a Christian is not easy at all. But the reward in the end is great. I am saved, sanctified, and holy ghost-filled, but at the end of the day I am a man who has much experience in the Christian walk. This is a lifestyle, a daily walk, and I hope my stories can give you inspiration in your walk, or even your hopes to begin a walk. This book is graphic, real, and words from an honest man of God. Enjoy!

More books available by Darick Spears on

www.darickbooks.com

And You Call Yourself a Christian by Darick Spears

Table of Contents

Church Hoe	Pg. 6
What in Hell You Want?	Pg. 13
Negative Annie	Pg. 17
Competition, Competition	Pg. 22
Sexuality Galaxy	Pg. 27
Divine Temple: Church Hurt	Pg. 36
Founder's Day	Pg. 57
The Death of a Ministry	Pg. 65
Agape love/ A-Gap-In-Love	Pg.74
Muzik: Microphone Check	Pg. 79
Sin Has No Weight	Pg. 84
And You Call Yourself Poem	Pg. 90
Let Me Be Me	Pg. 94

CHURCH HOE

And You Call Yourself a Christian by Darick Spears

It was a Sunday night, and church service had just let out. I was coming off a high from the service. It was the type of high where the spirit was moving in the church, and it consumed a lot of saints, and I caught only a contact from it. There were so many girls in church and my teenage hormones were going crazy. It was this beautiful girl that followed me out to my parent's car and was very helpful in helping me get some plates from the dinner earlier into the car.

It was dark outside but I had no worries at all. This girl was a quiet one, but in the dark, she reached for the middle part of my dress pants and began to feel on my private area. I had never experienced this rush, and after she pulled for a while, I felt so good I couldn't hold it in, and something came out of my private area. Later on in life, I would find out that I had my first orgasm at church. Was I guilty or intrigued? Honestly, I wanted it to happen again.

On the street's the definition of a hoe varies. Perhaps, there are women who sleep around with many men, or even men who sleep around with many women, that are considered hoes. Then the definition takes on another form, for a man or woman who is considered a punk or we call them hoe-ass folks. And if you are ever considered a hoe-

And You Call Yourself a Christian by Darick Spears

ass individual: then that is worse than being a hoe in my honest opinion.

Anyways, my definition of a church hoe extends beyond both of these. I would have to say that when a person comes to church just for the women or vice versa, and they sleep around a lot, then they would be considered a church hoe. I know because that was once me.

Getting your freak on in church was a big thing for youth coming up in my day. In the 90's, we would love when girls wore short skirts, and some even wore no panties underneath. This would be an easy way to feel your way around. I was the church drummer and that brought a little clout to my name, and traveling to different churches playing for my choir got me much attention. You see, when you are young, thinking this way isn't rare. But some of us get older and still think this way.

The church can be an exciting place to go, and one thing you must remember upon entrance is that everyone is not there for the same reasons. Some come to get their lives set in the right order. Others come because they need good people, (or they think), around them. Finally, there are some who come to get money from the church or even to get a companion(s).

I compare the church house to a hospital. The hospital is filled with sick and needy, thieves who are waiting for a member in their family to die to get their inheritance, and many other kinds.

The doctors, like Pastors, try their best to find solutions for sickness. But all in all, it can become very confusing for one who is just entering the building. So, you have to meet up with nurses, attendants who point you in the right direction, just to get a feel of the facility.

Back to the church hoe though; some don't realize they fall in this category until they take a check of themselves. It is okay to find a partner who shares the same faith, vision, and try to build a life with them; but when you are a Christian there are certain steps to the process.

Proverbs 18:22 states that He who finds a wife finds a good thing and obtains favor from the LORD.

So, all in all, it's not bad for a single man to find himself a wife, but sometimes when in search you can become what I call a church hoe. If you have dated, courted, 15 women or men in the course of a year; and slept with all or really any of them, then you can consider yourself a church hoe. The same goes for a woman.

Every day, I feel like it is appropriate to look in the mirror and ask myself, "Am I really a Christian?" I do it all the time. It is the examining of oneself, and not others that will get you right with God.

WHAT IN HELL YOU WANT?

One Sunday I was at church sitting in the back row, and my father was preaching. I was writing in my notebook as I usually do because I am a scribe. I have to record what goes on in my world and in the world today. My father spoke some words that not only got my immediate attention, but also all of the people in the church were attentive. He said, "What in hell you want?"

My father has always been a controversial preacher, because he speaks the direct truth. His words pierce when they come out. I have had friends who have gone to church with me for years tell me that they are afraid of my father. They say he is very real and they know he means business in the pulpit. But that day he made one of the most remarkable statements, that I feel should have been included in the beginning of the bible. He said, "What in hell you want?"

If you listen to that statement, it is actually a real question. What is it that a person is so anxious to have in hell? I don't know a person who wants to go to hell, go through hell, or be in hell; so, if you ask a person what in hell they want and they say nothing: then they should be trying their hardest to get on the path to heaven. It is that simple!

Some ask what the path to heaven is? It is quite simple, and I must tell you that it is through the bible. The bible is our weapon, our sword, our shield, and most importantly: it is the roadmap to heaven. Read it, study it, and apply it to your daily walk while building a personal relationship with Jesus Christ.

So, ask yourself in the mirror today, "What in hell you want?" I hope your answer is "Nothing at all!"

And You Call Yourself a Christian by Darick Spears

NEGATIVE ANNIE

Some days I just wake up completely negative. I don't feel like anything is going right, my breakthrough is a million miles away, and I am tired of everyone else having such incredible success. I don't even want to see anyone smile, laugh, and that spirit just affects my world. That is until I begin to analyze myself. Examining your own self is so effective. I begin to ask myself why I feel like this? Then I begin to look at all the checkpoints and easily I start dismissing the negativity.

And You Call Yourself a Christian by Darick Spears

I noticed that I had accomplished all of the tasks that I had written down on paper; and that I just needed to be more patient with my results. The bible talks about there is season for planting seeds, watering, and even enjoying the results. (Read Ecclesiastes 11:6) Sometimes it just takes time. I had been producing music, putting it out, and even traveling while winning awards. Success in the music industry is broken into different categories: fans, awards, money, etc.

At the time, I was very down and out, because I was receiving much accolades, fan mail, about my music; but I wanted to see more money, to make sure my methods were working. I prayed about it and was honest with God about how I felt. You see, when you pray you have to be completely honest with yourself and God. He must have heard my cry because I checked my account and it was a couple thousand dollars in there, that wasn't there before. I traced it back, and it was a royalty check from just one of my songs.

I have hundreds of songs out there, and this was just from one. I instantly realized something; and that was that in due season I would be reaping millions of dollars from my songs if I just remained patient and hard-working. I made sure to create, and own my entire catalogs of music and writings, and whatever I do. People laugh and tell me I am crazy for putting out so much material.

But I don't do it for the cash, and I don't let cash stop me from doing what I do. I believe that one day everything I put out will sell millions and

And You Call Yourself a Christian by Darick Spears

affect in a positive manner everyone who comes across my catalog. I do it because I am inspired by God, by life, and by all the gifts God has given me. I had to remember this as I continued my day that started off bad.

My attitude instantly changed from being negative to positive. You see, sometimes you have to just analyze your situation, see if you've done all you can, and just be patient. You build it, and it will come. Work hard, don't miss a step, and trust in God.

Competition, Competition!!!

And You Call Yourself a Christian by Darick Spears

Many times, growing up in a church family creates a competitive monster. Don't let anyone tell you differently, when I say that church folks are just plain "competitive."

From the choir director trying to out due the visiting church's choir director, to every member on the praise team fighting to get the mic, and even the minster trying to out preach the Pastor: everyone becomes competitive. This is why most lose Jesus and the meaning of being a true Christian in the process.

Growing up, we made everything about competition. From, the way we dressed at church to who could shout (dance), the best, was just a piece of the competition. You see, if you are not familiar with what shouting is, then I am sure you could find a Youtube video that shows church music playing and people running up and down the church dancing, and praising God. Some movies have been made actually showing the comical side of church shouting.

But like sororities and fraternities with their stepping: people in the church take shouting very seriously; and sometimes you may see two people on the floor at a time going hard. Some may wonder if they are actually trying to out due each other, or if they are seriously praising God? That's between them and God.

I didn't like all the competition because it created too much tension, and it was hard to find anyone or any deed sincere. When someone befriended you in the church, was it to make another person jealous? I know this may seem

And You Call Yourself a Christian by Darick Spears

petty, but it is actually very true and happens all the time. We become like pawns in someone's chess game.

I have seen people attend the same church and claim to love the same God but would not speak to a saint at the church for a year straight because of a competitive attitude. You tell me if that is a part of God's nature?

In sports, competition makes teams better, it makes coaches better, and it makes the leagues better. However, players still learn to get along with one another after the game is done, and some even become best of friends. But they compete for the love of the game. When we do it in church, it really doesn't belong there.

"Jesus said unto him, "Thou shalt love the Lord thy God with all thy heart, and with all thy soul, and with all thy mind." This is the first and great commandment. And the second is like unto it, "Thou shalt love thy neighbor as thyself." On these two commandments hang all the law and the prophets."
_ Matthew 22:36-40

Within those commandments, competition is irrelevant. Honestly, it doesn't belong in the church because we are all technically going for the same thing. That is to obtain mercy, forgiveness, salvation, the holy ghost, guidance, and to proclaim the word of God to those in need.

And You Call Yourself a Christian by Darick Spears

SEXUALITY GALAXY

Are you struggling with your true sexuality? Or are you just struggling with sexual tension in your body, and feel like no one gets it? Well I'm here to tell you that it's natural to feel horny. It's natural to see an attractive person and wonder things. But there is a problem finding yourself lusting; moving beyond a thought into a galaxy of playing out your fantasy.

The plain truth is that God made man for woman. I'm sorry to burst your fantasy bubble, when you begin to think that a man was made for a man, or a woman for a woman.

Look at evolution period. How could we populate the earth with two men? Or with two women? Two dicks together will not produce a baby, nor will two vaginas together make a baby.

And You Call Yourself a Christian by Darick Spears

This is the most commonsense thing that God probably ever made as an equation. A man and a woman have two different parts that actual fit together, and when they unite they produce a seed that grows into a baby. Wow!! Commonsense right?

Well for some people, and it seems like for a lot of people now-a-days; they want the total opposite. That is just a sexual spirit that comes from the underworld that has been stroking this world for many centuries. Now it is so prevalent, and people are trying to push it into religion.

I have to be totally honest, as a person who has made it my destiny to walk this Christian race; it doesn't belong in your Christian walk. Why? Why? Some may ask me, and my answer is very simple: "Because the Bible says so."

You see, Christians have a manual to follow called the Bible. Within it, are the various rules, regulations, just as if you were joining the military or a new job, that we must abide by. So, when I tell you that lusting is a sin I can refer to:

Matthew 5:28 English Standard Version (ESV)

²⁸ But I say to you that everyone who looks at a woman with lustful intent has already committed adultery with her in his heart.

Or even-

1 Corinthians 6:18 English Standard Version (ESV)

¹⁸ Flee from sexual immorality. Every other sin[a] a person commits is outside the body, but the sexually immoral person sins against his own body.

When I need answers about homosexuality within the Christian and why it occurs I can refer to

And You Call Yourself a Christian by Darick Spears

Romans 1:26-28

26 Because of this, God gave them over to shameful lusts. Even their women exchanged natural sexual relations for unnatural ones.

27 In the same way the men also abandoned natural relations with women and were inflamed with lust for one another. Men committed shameful acts with other men, and received in themselves the due penalty for their error.

28 Furthermore, just as they did not think it worthwhile to retain the knowledge of God, so God gave them over to a depraved mind, so that they do what ought not to be done.

1 Corinthians 6:9-11

9 Or do you not know that wrongdoers will not inherit the kingdom of God? Do not be deceived:

Neither the sexually immoral nor idolaters nor adulterers nor men who have sex with men

10 nor thieves nor the greedy nor drunkards nor slanderers nor swindlers will inherit the kingdom of God.

11And that is what some of you were. But you were washed, you were sanctified, you were justified in the name of the Lord Jesus Christ and by the Spirit of our God.

1 Timothy 1:8-11

8 We know that the law is good if one uses it properly.

9 We also know that the law is made not for the righteous but for lawbreakers and rebels, the ungodly and sinful, the unholy and irreligious, for those who kill their fathers or mothers, for murderers,

And You Call Yourself a Christian by Darick Spears

10 for the sexually immoral, for those practicing homosexuality, for slave traders and liars and perjurers—and for whatever else is contrary to the sound doctrine
11 that conforms to the gospel concerning the glory of the blessed God, which he entrusted to me.

The great thing about God is that he gives us free will. You can do the right thing, or you can do the wrong thing. But there are always consequences whether good or bad.

I love the bible because it is a study guide. It has many stories, warnings, prophecies, and much more that help us move from a natural walk to a spiritual walk. It's not always easy being a Christian because people don't understand the lifestyle, or the movement. They don't think we struggle with things like lust, envy, etc.

But the awesome thing that separates a Christian from the entire world is that we strive every day to please God and not our flesh, we push even harder to depend solely on God; and we are the true salt of the earth. Imagine eating a piece of meat without any salt on it and you will find it bland. But add some salt and the flavor comes out. That's what Christians are to the world.

So, I know you are struggling with something, and you even find yourself in the dark uncomfortable with the situation.

That is because it probably doesn't fit you, and deep down inside you know it isn't right. I tell you to drop to your knees and pray about it and ask God for true guidance and be obedient to his word.

And You Call Yourself a Christian by Darick Spears

It will only lead you to eternal life. All are welcome into the house of God to be cleansed, and rebuilt through his word, his baptism, and his holy spirit.

The spirit will not enter into a filthy temple, so you must be clean. Confess your faults to God, ask for forgiveness and get onto your journey.

This chapter is only for those who want to truly walk the Christian walk. For the ones who don't want to pursue a Christian lifestyle, this isn't for you, but I hope you consider one day!

Divine Temple:

Church Hurt

And You Call Yourself a Christian by Darick Spears

(This is NOT a Dis Chapter: It is a Real Chapter)

Church hurt is the worst hurt. This is because when you are around individuals who claim to be Christ-like, or even your church family; you don't expect back-stabbing and falseness. But this happens even on the streets, they just deal with it differently. I like to write about my own experiences, and I only speak for myself. This is my Divine Temple paraphrased story.

My family and I, headed by my father Pastor Dennis Spears Sr., were in a transition of leaving our prior church Power House of Deliverance, and starting our own ministry. During this time, we were like many churches that were just starting up in the 90's: we were having service in our basement. As a teenager, it is funny at first having church in the house, but eventually you realize how serious your parents are about the ministry.

That could also come with so many unwanted responsibilities. This is because people who go to church are always trying to keep up an image. I am not speaking for everyone in the world, but I am speaking for myself and the church world that I was raised in. It makes me laugh at how many so-called Christians claim to serve a God that is almighty, yet they act like cowards.

I saw so many people who came to church on Sunday, Wednesday, Friday, and would consume so much of the word of God; and in the same light they would be scared of their own community.

And You Call Yourself a Christian by Darick Spears

You would think that if someone received the Good News, they would want to be amongst the people who would benefit from the good news? Instead, church folks congregate in the same buildings and circles, and tear each other down. At Divine Temple, it was no different!

Divine Temple was started by two families, the Great Pastor Otha Howard and his wife, and Bishop Charles Dickens and his beautiful wife Linda Dickens in about 1995. I don't have the exact date, because this isn't a history paper; it's just my recollection. My family and I came to the church in 1996, and we were there until the death of the Late Great Pastor Otha Howard in mid-2017.

My parents stood by Pastor Howard through the thick and thin. Even though the Co-Pastoring relationship eventually dissolved between Pastor Howard and Bishop Dickens, we stood by Pastor Howard. The real truth is that the church split in half. A lot of my church friends, who I considered family, and still do, went with Bishop Dickens and the beautiful Linda Dickens, and they started a church called Victory Temple.

It got bad for a while, and probably never healed, because attitudes were developed between the two churches. I saw it with my own eyes. I was cool with both sides, and I heard from people's mouths, their grief towards one another. I was confused at this time, and was in the forefront of the youth, that were my age left at Divine.

And You Call Yourself a Christian by Darick Spears

A lot of the other youth were younger at Divine Temple, and my sister Latoya and I, were amongst the older youth that stayed. My father was a true soldier for Pastor Otha Howard. I would get angry sometimes, by how much loyalty he had for him.

If Pastor Howard didn't like a certain hairstyle, my mom and dad would make sure we didn't have it. They were all about loyalty and respect. If anyone wonders where I get my loyalty from, it comes from my parents. They are loyal people.

They do not talk about people behind their backs. They love all, and they also fear none. A lot of kids may hear their parents at home talking poorly about people from the church, and then they see their parents hugging them at church the next Sunday.

That's fake, and I never saw that in my household. If my brothers or sister tell you anything differently, then they are liars and should be smacked. I grew up in a very strict Christ-like home. The only difference is, that my parents always allowed me to be myself. I am very bold and outspoken, and people have always reacted to that in either fear, or confusion. My parents learned to let me be me. But they would let me know if I was going too far. They are big on respecting everyone, but not letting someone walk over you. I use the same tactics with my kids.

After the church split, my father stood by Pastor Otha Howard, and he wouldn't let him hit the floor, even if he was falling himself. They built the

And You Call Yourself a Christian by Darick Spears

church up together, and I watched it every step, while also contributing. You see, the youth at Divine Temple, also put in work to help build the church. Everyone in a church who goes and is a member, should play a part in building the ministry. If you're not, then you should "slap yourself."

I could write a whole book on Divine Temple, but this book is more than my experience at this church. However, I created this chapter to speak on something that most churches go through, and many people don't have the forums that I have to tell it, and that is called "church hurt."

My father was Assistant Pastor at Divine Temple for 15-plus years, and he prided himself in helping Pastor Howard fulfill his vision.

I mean, I would watch my dad be protective of Pastor Howard, like he was his own father.

(Footnote: my dad never had a relationship with his biological father, and we never had a grandfather on my dad's side). They were spiritually married in the word of God, and they had the same vision. Pastor Howard understood my father, and my father understood him. My dad is the most honest and direct individual I know, besides myself of course. But that's where I get it from.

When it comes to church, people in the audience who we call members, are often very sensitive. The reason they are, is because most of them are living in sin; and Pastor Howard and my father attacked sin all the time. There were other men in the supporting cast that came eventually, and some were there from the beginning.

One in particular was his son Calvin Howard, who was really just over the music department. He,

And You Call Yourself a Christian by Darick Spears

and his wife Michele, were the heads of the youth department, and we spent a lot of time with this family. Us young people, would be over their house all of the time, and we went on youth outings and had a ball. I was very close with Michele and even referred to her as my second mom. I cannot ever say anything bad about Michele, because she has only been a good person to me.

Everyone called Calvin "Chuck", and we always just thought of him as the organ player. The youth often loved when he got up to preach, because we all would be in the back laughing at our 5-minute timer. We called him the 5-minute preacher, because he only spoke for less than 5 minutes.

Even his own kids would say this. It was no disrespect to him, because it was the truth. Chuck worked with the youth, and Michele, and they did a great job. But when it came to the spiritual building of the church, and the real-down to business preaching and teaching we only looked for two people to do it: Pastor Otha Howard & Assistant Pastor Spears. If anyone tells you differently, then may God strike them down.

Divine Temple was at one point a little building full of love, fun, and family. Then as time passed, Pastor Howard's vision to expand the building pushed into play, and even then, we were all a little family supporting our Pastor.

We had other church affiliations to an extent. We would fellowship with St. Paul, Johnson Temple, and other churches; but we were our own island. Pastor Howard had been through church hurt before

And You Call Yourself a Christian by Darick Spears

he started Divine Temple, and he being a trailblazer, started his own establishment called Divine Temple.

Other churches didn't have input on how we did things at our church, and we had one Pastor, and one Assistant Pastor. After the dissolving of Divine Temple, and Victory Temple; Pastor Howard didn't believe in the Two-Headed Monster. You see, Partnerships usually end in bad terms anyways.

This is because the power structure is even, and one person may not agree with what the other person is doing, and a split is caused. When this is a church situation, people will follow one leader and rebel against the other.

So, now Pastor Howard was the solo leader, and he had my father as the Assistant up until his death. Divine Temple started its expansion, and things began to change. Sometimes bigger is not better, and in my honest opinion, if Divine Temple stayed small, we would all still be together. All of a sudden, people started to help with donations, help with inside the building work; and it felt great to see everyone working together, but snakes aren't always seen in the beginning.

I watched Pastor Howard come in to see the church getting done, while holding his air machine. He had grown sick and was unable to lead the church like he usually would. My father assumed the Assistant/Pastor role while our leader fought to get back healthy. Divine Temple would fellowship with the then Johnson Temple for over a year's period of time.

I watched Chuck push to help get his father's vision done physically. Always showing up and putting in a lot of work for his father. He was a tremendous help and leading force in the actual building get done, and we all helped anytime he

And You Call Yourself a Christian by Darick Spears

called. Everyone was helping in their own way. My father was doing the spiritual work and helping with the natural as well with Chuck. During this period of time, I had gained a new respect for Chuck, but I would soon lose it all. You see, the devil comes to "lie, steal, kill, and destroy."

I witnessed people beginning to act funny. A lot came from newer people at the church, who weren't there from the beginning, and who carried a conditional attitude. People who have conditional attitudes, only do things for you with a condition behind it. For example, they will give you money towards your church only if they get an input on your sermons.

Others will find and appoint themselves roles and titles that they don't even qualify for, only because they feel their conditional attitudes grant that. Divine Temple, like many other churches and organizations, fell victim to this. Elders in the church who felt they supported the Pastor's vision financially, thought they should be successors. Attitudes began to surface and show up as the building entered into its completion. I began to wish we never expanded.

No one was even thinking of running Divine Temple, until the new building arrived. But sometimes I wondered, "were they always going for that spot that Pastor Howard and Assistant Pastor Spears were called and ordained for?" I personally would never want to hold any positions in the church. I just want to be a vessel, and do whatever God leads me to do.

But there are some sick individuals who hunger after power, and don't understand the amount of work it takes to be a Pastor or an

And You Call Yourself a Christian by Darick Spears

Assistant Pastor. You will be judged by your title by both man and God. You should only be worried about God's judgment concerning your work, and this is because if you don't tell them the truth; even if it hurts their feelings, or even makes them uncomfortable: then God will punish you.

Pastor Howard never bit his tongue, and I always loved and respected him for this. I didn't always agree with what he said, or even obeyed what he said. I used to go out and drink, have sex, and all kinds of other things and then go to church. But I never played church, or with God.

I sat my butt down and repented; and I got it right before I continued. One thing I knew was the truth, and that was because Pastor Howard and Assistant Pastor Spears taught it.

If you've noticed, I always put them on the same line because they worked together like a good parenting relationship. Pastor Howard would tell my father, "NEVER APLOGIZE FOR A MESSAGE THAT GOD GAVE YOU TO SPEAK."

It was times that my dad would speak to Pastor Howard in private to make sure he didn't go to hard while preaching, and Pastor Howard would tell him not to apologize about something God gave him to say. Pastor Howard was the same way, and he was really a true man of God.

Divine Temple had reached its goal of being able to open its doors and have church; but there was still work that needed to be done before the building could be considered completed. I remember the opening service, and this is because I filmed it. I saw Pastor Howard coming up those stairs with that look on his face, that showed he was

And You Call Yourself a Christian by Darick Spears

tired physically, but proud of his accomplishments. He gave his last sermon that night, and walked around the church with his wife.

As I filmed, I knew in my heart that he didn't have much time left, and I was saddened. Divine Temple's history just ran through my head like a sped-up cassette tape, and I wanted to cry, while everyone else was rejoicing. I looked around the church and saw the same people who had hurt Pastor Howard in the past, the same ones who would hurt his legacy in the future, all in one room. I wondered if he could see this as well.

Pastor Howard passed away about a month later, and all hell broke loose. Divine Temple, as I said before was its own entity, and once Pastor Howard passed, it became everyone else's entity.

The weak and the snakes began to show up. My father was torn up. He didn't want to be Pastor. He wanted Pastor Howard to live longer so he could keep supporting him. He took pride in serving, and it was his time to step up to do what Pastor Howard had wanted him to do. Mother Howard, spoke to my father after Pastor Howard passed, and said that she was going to follow my father, because that's what her husband's wishes were.

Chuck Howard and his brother Dale did and said the same. My father was asked to preach the funeral, and it was the most difficult thing he had to do. I had never seen my father in this state before, but he was so hurt.

He loved Pastor Howard so much, that when Chuck Howard began to plot against my father to be the Pastor; my dad didn't fight him over it. People don't know how deep my father respects Pastor

Howard. Other preachers felt like they should have preached the funeral, but they weren't even there for Pastor Howard at his lowest point; they were only there during high points, or anniversaries.

People started to show their true colors and their conditional attitudes. The one's who gave money to help build the new church now felt like they could all of a sudden call the shots; and they began to feed Chuck's ears with complaints about my dad being too strict of a Pastor. The bible talks about individuals sowing discord amongst the brethren.

Romans 16:17-18 English Standard Version (ESV)

[17] I appeal to you, brothers, to watch out for those who cause divisions and create obstacles contrary to the doctrine that you have been taught; avoid them. [18] For such persons do not serve our Lord

Christ, but their own appetites,[a] and by smooth talk and flattery they deceive the hearts of the naive.

The complainers picked the right one to get on board with this, and it was Chuck.

Chuck has never been through the history of Divine Temple, a spiritual leader. He was only a youth leader. He has never been one you would go to for prayer, for teaching of the bible, etc. He was always great at helping with the church landscape, and whatever other things needed to be done, as a deacon would do.

So, when it came time for people to voice their opinions about Divine Temple, they went to Chuck, and eventually he began to do something that in two weeks would destroy what his father had built.

And You Call Yourself a Christian by Darick Spears

FOUNDERS DAY SERVICE

After the late-Great Pastor Howard went on to glory, Divine Temple had a Founder's Day service that was supposed to show appreciation to the Founders of The Church of The First Born. But that Sunday of the Founder's Day service was all craziness. It was so many bad attitudes within the Divine Temple organization. No one wanted to work together and I could feel it in my spirit that it just was not right. I watched from the sound board that I was controlling during service.

You could cut the tension with a knife, and you could clearly see the disrespect of other elders in the church. Since Pastor Howard had passed, none of these elders wanted to show any type of respect towards Pastor Spears. They were trying to walk over him indirectly, and sometimes I felt directly.

The Founders day dinner was supposed to begin by about 1 p.m. and my father had two of the elders get up to have words, and after that the protocol would be for them to give the mic over to him to complete the service. Instead, one of the elders got up and literally spoke until 1:10 p.m. and tried to do an alter call like he had no respect for the

And You Call Yourself a Christian by Darick Spears

Pastor's wishes. Many people were looking confused. It was not looking good, and the beginning of the ending had started.

I was hurt, and I honestly was done with Divine Temple at that moment, because I could see what the spirit of competition had done to the people. It was no longer about the elders wanting to see the people saved, it was about who could run the church better.

It was sick to watch, and my spirit was stirred up. It had gotten even worst when the Founders day dinner started. No one in the kitchen wanted anyone else's help. We had a bigger church and it took twice as long for the food to get served than it did when we had a smaller building. I could feel the spirit of God leading me to observe all of these things.

It's like he was guiding me around the church to watch what was happening. I began to get frustrated. One of my gifts is fearlessness and truth-speaking; and I believe God knew what he was doing by showing me these things.

He showed me the disrespectfulness of the elders, and how they were trying to walk over the Pastor Spears.

He showed me that Satan had entered and the confusion, jealousy, and separation traps that had already been in the hearts of these people, were now surfacing. It was about to get ugly. There was no order, and there was a war going on in the church that Pastor Spears did not even have to fight. God would give him a message, which would be his final one at Divine Temple in the weeks to come.

And You Call Yourself a Christian by Darick Spears

I sat in deep observation, and even as the afternoon service went on I watched all these visiting churches, family members who had stuck around for weeks after the funeral, just to be nosey. I whispered to God to allow me an opportunity to say something as the service ended, and my moment came.

I know it was God that gave me the opportunity to put some order back into the church. As I stood up, I acknowledged the late-Great Pastor Howard, and then I moved on to acknowledge our Pastor Spears.

As I said it I heard a voice in the audience yell, "Assistant, Assistant." This person was not even a member of Divine Temple, and all that God had shown me about all of the attitudes, tension, nosey family members sticking around; came out instantly and would show up even more in the next weeks. It was actually Pastor Howards brother who had said "Assistant, Assistant."

I had been at Divine Temple for 20 plus years and I had never known him to be even a member. I never saw him by Pastor Howard's side during those years at Divine Temple, and Pastor Howard was the one who made Pastor Spears his successor.

So, I felt like that was a slap to Pastor Howards face when his brother said that. Might I mind you, all I ever spoke was the truth at the Founder's Day. I just acknowledged my father as the Pastor, because he was in fact the Pastor. It was nothing but God through me, putting order back in the church. You see, when a President dies, or a CEO dies, their successor takes immediate position

And You Call Yourself a Christian by Darick Spears

as the head of the country or company; or else order would go crazy.

So, God was saying through my words, that the people of Divine Temple have a Pastor and they need to respect the man of God that he himself looks at as the new Angel of The Church.

Instead people from other churches rebelled, and they didn't even have a right or a say-so in something they never helped to build. After I spoke at the Founders Day service for about a brief minute, I went directly up to Chuck Howard as he sat on his piano and asked him, "did I say anything wrong up there?" He looked me dead in my eyes and said "No, not at all!"

After I spoke to Chuck, I walked to directly up to Pastor Howards brother and looked him dead in his eyes, and said, "nothing I said was meant to be disrespectful, and he said it was ok." So, I felt like all was ok. But it wasn't because even until this day, Chuck and every other little mouse that's afraid to say things directly to me, claims that I caused a lot of calamity at Divine temple by what I said at the Founder's Day service.

What they fail to see, is that God spoke twice to Divine Temple before the true death of their ministry. He spoke through me to get back the true order of respect in the church during the Founders Day, and weeks later he would speak through my father Pastor Spears about discord, disrespect, and others not following true Sound Doctrine.

And You Call Yourself a Christian by Darick Spears

The Death of a Ministry/Legacy

After the Founders Day service, I don't even know if Chuck noticed what he was doing, and until this day he may not but I will show him. He would call my father weekly with reports that either the church documents had been stolen, or that one of the Elder's at the church family was trying to steal the church. Then the next week it was another family trying to steal the church, and what it began to do was create divisions.

He was never bringing the Meeks or the Roberson's or the Spears's into one room so they all could talk. Instead, he would call my father and play pass the message about what someone else said about him. My dad has never been a gossip person, and he doesn't do those things. Chuck does, and did in fact cause so much division that he left people hearing half of a story and not knowing the other half.

You see, a liar never wants all parties involved in a lie to all be in the room at the same time. It would benefit a liar to keep them all separate. Remember, the devil comes to "lie, kill, steal, and destroy."

And You Call Yourself a Christian by Darick Spears

St. Paul, Johnson Temple, and all types of other churches were now putting their input on how Divine Temple was being ran. I wondered was this payback for the way some Divine Temple members treated Victory Temple members in the past. We became the talk, and I began receiving phone calls from some of my friends about what they were hearing at their church, and it was all coming from Chuck.

In the midst of this storm, my father did what he and Pastor Howard has always done, "preached the real word." But this time after his message Chuck approached him and said if he keeps preaching like that, then the only people who will be left in Divine Temple would be his family and my dad's family. The devil had spoken and shown his face.

Divine Temple was now a different organization that Pastor Howard would have not even approved of. This is the same Pastor who told my father to "never apologize for a message God had given you." Now, his own son was saying the opposite? My father could sense that it was time to go, and Chuck did what only a coward would do.

He called my sister Latoya to ask her to call my father to see if they could talk. Must I remind you that Chuck had been calling my father prior to that for weeks, for years at the same number. So, after my sister reached out to my father, he told Chuck sure they could meet at my dad's house and talk.

And You Call Yourself a Christian by Darick Spears

Chuck agreed, but then decided not to show up, but rather call my father over the phone. He told him that he would be assuming role of Pastor and didn't need an assistant. After this my father and mother left Divine Temple, and NEVER encouraged anyone else to leave with them. That was the official day that the spiritual side of Divine Temple died. Divine Temple was spiritually built by Pastor Otha Howard, and Assistant Pastor Spears. These were the spiritual partners who built and carried the church.

That place will never be the same, and to be honest until Chuck Howard and the people their open their eyes and repent, it won't exist.

My reaction to all of this was to let the people know the truth, without sounding petty. Chuck Howards kids, who I once considered my little brothers and sisters got suckered into believing the non-sense. It's sad how when someone dies, we all act like we listened and respected everything that the person wanted us to do. I already spoke for myself saying I didn't always do and respect Pastor Howards wishes, but I did love and support the ministry. I don't know if they can honestly say the same. And they would liars if they said they always did......

I begged my dad to let me speak on his behalf about what really happened, and this is because in your absence anyone can tell your story. So, he allowed me to let the people know the truth. I put a video out, and in about one hour's time, it caused a bit of a storm. To be honest, that was just the beginning for me. I was fighting for my father and Pastor Howard. I watched them build this, and

Chuck was and is a perpetrator, and a vessel used to destroy.

My personal feelings intervened as I spoke to God and told him that I felt like Chuck had no Holy Ghost, no wisdom, or leadership. I am not one who can judge Chuck, but I do feel anyone who can read all of this and still follow him, is just as blind as he is. I pray that God opens his eyes, and others around him.

I miss the small building that Divine Temple used to have, because it was real love there. We would sell dinners in the basement and be squashed together because it was hardly any room, but we had love.

A lot of people are hurt, and they are blind to the truth. I have not given anyone any lies in this chapter. It is all the truth, and what you do with the truth you are given, defines your character in the end.

James 4:17 says If anyone, then, knows the good they ought to do and doesn't do it, it is sin for them. I therefore have given you the truth and the reason I left Divine Temple, because I won't follow what is not right. That defines my character, what about yours?

And You Call Yourself a Christian by Darick Spears

Pastor Howard, I put this chapter together to show you respect and to respect the bible which tells me "Open rebuke is better than secret love."_ Proverbs 27:5

I hope you liked the documentary I put together for you! It was from the heart! You were a special man, and I know you were a true man of God. My father and mother have always loved and respected you. The things that happened after your passing were beyond your control. But I am glad God sent us to help with Divine Temple, and we have moved on. It's time we gave the world "Sound Doctrine Outreach Ministries," and I'm sure you already know Pastor Dennis Spears Sr. will preach and teach the truth until he meets you again in heaven. And trust me, I will be there too!

Agape love/ (A-Gap-In-Love)

And You Call Yourself a Christian by Darick Spears

My grandmother, Mary Hill, is one of the best people I know. She has a heart of pure gold, and her love is always shown. I watch her give her all to people all the time. She just loves to give. It makes her feel good, and I know God smiles down on her every day. I wish all people could be like her. She has no agenda when she loves.

A lot of people don't even show her the same love back, but I know I do. I love her and will always love her, because she is the one example of the purest love that I have ever seen with my eye. It is no wonder why I have such a great-loving mother.

I could write a whole book about my grandmother Mary Hill, and all the lessons and stories she has taught me. But I cherish those and keep them bottled close to my heart. If you haven't gotten to know her, then you should!

Love is an action word. If someone really loves you, they honestly never need to say it to you, because it is their actions that tell the true story. When a person has to constantly tell you that they love you, it is because they may be trying to not only convince you that they love you; but also, convince themselves.

Church people are the worst when it comes to this. After my family and I left Divine Temple, the same people who had our phone numbers for years, somehow forgot that our phones still worked. Yet, when they would run into one of us in public, the first thing they would say is "You know I still love y'all and miss y'all." Those were complete lies, and they were just phony people trying to convince themselves that they loved us.

And You Call Yourself a Christian by Darick Spears

The reason a lot of people feel like Jesus is not real, and that he doesn't love them is because the individuals who are in the church give a false representation.

They are evil, they are crooked, they are not full of love at all (and I am not speaking for all): and when someone who is trying to get know Jesus through the church that they attend, finds fake love, back-stabbing, a false prophet; they immediately associate it with Jesus.

This is terrible. My advice to anyone who goes to church, or wants to go to church, is to build a personal relationship with Jesus yourself.

Don't depend on the Pastor to give you a relationship with Jesus, or the deacon, or missionary. This is because they are just normal people like you, and they too are trying to get to heaven. Well, some of them!!!

The foundation of the Christian walk is purely built on love. Jesus went to the cross and died for the sins of the world, forgave those who persecuted him, and still gave the believers a right to the tree of life.

That is love! Whenever we say we can't forgive our neighbor, we have been treated so wrong, we are tired of being gossiped about, and much more: all we have to do is look at the entire scene of Jesus on the cross, and redirect or focus on true Agape Love.

And You Call Yourself a Christian by Darick Spears

Muzik: Microphone Check

Music is a gift from God. Can you honestly imagine the world without any music? It would be pure boredom and it would be meaningless. I would like to take this time to write about the music influence in church, and how so many people are totally wrong about music and lyrics.

First of all, as a true poet and musician I would like to say that unless you have listened to a complete album, a complete catalog of someone's music, or even asked them personally what's the meaning behind their song: it's disrespectful to judge their music.

As I have grown up in church, I have heard so many people name drop an artist, and talk badly about their music, and how they devil worship, or how hip hop is the devil's music, jazz, rock n roll,

And You Call Yourself a Christian by Darick Spears

etc. When the truth of the matter is that the Bible or the Christian walk doesn't much apply to a person who has not chosen that walk as a lifestyle.

Equally important, I have gotten more honesty from a Tupac Album, or Marvin Gaye's "What Going On album," than I have from 95% of the preachers who speak in the pulpit. When I write my music, I write from the heart.

The true artists are brave and speak on what's really going on in the world. When little kids are getting raped, killed by police; our lyrics might say that the situation is "Fucked up." The reason we say that is because we put ourselves in the shoes of the other person, and we combine it with our emotion, and speak the direct truth, for ourselves and for the people.

Instantly, church people want to judge because of the language, and the truth is language evolves, and new words are made up every day. I believe what you speak in truth, at the same time combined with your true emotion, is considered "real." The way you say something gives it different meaning.

I could see my friend and shake his hand, hug him and say "My nigga," and he accepts it in a loving manner. Now if I walked passed him and didn't shake his hand and just say "Nigga," he going to take that as a dis or a feeling of disrespect. A lot of times it's the action that comes with something that gives words power. Church people get on my nerves.

And You Call Yourself a Christian by Darick Spears

They talk about all of these genres and forget that the same person who wrote the gospel song that they sing daily is struggling with homosexuality.

There is no such thing as Gospel Hip Hop. Those two are separate cultures, and lifestyles. I think people who say Gospel Hip Hop, are churchy people who want to be cool, that don't do the research or actually live the culture of Hip Hop.

This chapter is just a quick microphone check to all the people who judge my music and others, and don't know the true meaning about or behind what we do. Respect it and never judge it!

Sin has No Weight

And You Call Yourself a Christian by Darick Spears

Sin itself is a heavy weight that no one who is a Christian wants to have. It keeps your spiritual man heavy and the truth is that we should always try to keep our temples clean. Our spiritual man is very important, because it is what we take with us when we leave this world. We will not take our natural bodies with us, because we believe as Christians that we will receive a new spiritual body.

1 Corinthians 15:44

They are buried as natural human bodies, but they will be raised as spiritual bodies. For just as there are natural bodies, there are also spiritual bodies.

So, it is important for us to stay as sin free as possible. But I would like to explain the phrase I use "Sin has no weight." What I mean by this is the weight we put on sin. We compare our own sins to others, so that we feel like we have done less wrong than someone else.

I try to never do this, because wrong is wrong, and sin is a sin in God's eyes. There are only two sins that the Bible speaks of that are not forgiven by God: those are blasphemy against the holy ghost and suicide.

Mark 3:28-30:

"Truly I tell you, all sins and blasphemes will be forgiven for the sons of men. But whoever blasphemes against the Holy Spirit will never be forgiven but is guilty of an eternal sin. He said this because they [the Pharisees] were saying, 'He has an evil spirit'."

Now one may ask how suicide can't be forgiven and I will tell you. After the death is the judgement. there is no other chance.

Hebrews 9: 27

    Just as man is appointed to die once, and after that to face judgment,

2 Corinthians 5:10

    For we must all appear before the judgment seat of Christ, that each one may receive his due for the things done in the body, whether good or bad.

    It is true that killing yourself is a sin and you can't ask for forgiveness once you're already dead. The bible says "Thou shalt not kill." Exodus 20:13

    But as far as every other sin, it is sin in God's eyes. It is all wrong! So, if you are judging a man for cheating on his wife, but at the same time you are lusting after someone in your heart: you are just as guilty as he is. If you have stolen and you look at the man who has killed, and you feel better about your sin: you must realize you are both sinners in God's eyes.

Man puts weight on sin, and to be honest in God's eyes unless you have blasphemed against the Holy Ghost or committed suicide: you can be forgiven of those sins. A murderer and a fornicator can be forgiven and still have the right to the tree of life.

Stop feeling like your sin is any less of a sin than anybody else's. Daily self-examination will surely get you on the righteous path,

And You Call Yourself a Christian by Darick Spears

because you will be more concerned about your soul.

Sin has No Weight!

And You Call Yourself a Christian:

A Poem of Examination to Myself

The Questions

So, Darick you call yourself a Christian?
You think corrupt sometimes,
You've indulged in lust at times,
You've even ruffed up some niggas who wouldn't listen.
Cheated on your wife,
And yet you call yourself a Christian?

You didn't have to slam that dudes head into the mirror that one time,
You didn't have push that dude down the steps,

And You Call Yourself a Christian by Darick Spears

You didn't have stand up to the bouncers for your 98.3 crew that one time,
You didn't have to at age 15 write suicide letters to yourself.

So, Darick you call yourself a Christian?
How does it feel to try so hard and keep on slipping?
How did it feel when the kids in your class kept laughing and calling you different?
How did it feel when you beat up half of your white friends growing up,
Just cuz they kept calling you a nigger?

You go through so much and how are you always all smiles?

I can't stand you!
It's like you have this eternal resilience.
I hear people call you stupid all the time,
You're crazy if you even think you're brilliant.

Why do you always feel you have to tell the truth?
How do you get older yet keep so much youth?

You call yourself a Christian,
But people who go to church think you're a demon,
They hate your music,
They think your lyrics are inappropriate and misleading.

But why does God keep blessing you?
Why does he have so much favor in you?
Why does he forgive you for your shortcomings?
Why is he the only one who doesn't think you're a dummy?
Why does he show you these visions?
He inspires you to write books like this one?
He gives you messages to tell others even when you think nobody is going to listen?

My Reply

My reply to all your questions is as simple as this,

The Lord knows my heart.

I try and give my all in all that I do.

Negative spirit: You are not me, and I am not you!

I am only a man who has accepted Jesus in my life.

And You Call Yourself a Christian by Darick Spears

Just by accepting him, doesn't mean I will do everything right.
I won't say everything precise.
My job daily is to examine myself.
I honestly wrote this book as an assessment of my own life and self.
When I see Jesus on the day of judgment I can't speak for anyone else.
I promise to keep searching,
Keep running in this Christian race even if my legs are hurting,
Keep bouncing back when my decisions show you that I'm not perfect,
Because one day I will hear Jesus say,

"Well –done my good and faithful servant!."

LET ME BE ME

And You Call Yourself a Christian by Darick Spears

To the children of the church it is very necessary that you be who you are. That is in personality and awkward fashion. What I mean by this is that God truly created every individual as an individual. He made no two alike. The church has suppressed many of the people that walk through its doors. This is because they have the word uniform misunderstood.

The Bible tells us to let this same mind be in you that was in Christ Jesus (Phillipians 2:5). The only one we should pattern our mind and walk like is God. Too many times we enter into church and try to become a carbon copy of another evangelist, minister, usher, in the church; instead of bringing our own flavor to the table that God gave us.

Don't be afraid to present your new ideas, your fashion, etc. But remember to let all things be done decently and in order (1 Corithians 14:40). Study your bible every day, because a lot of times things said in the church are purely opinions, and you can begin to find yourself being imprisoned by opinions.

Set yourself free today from snares, opinions, and the cloning of someone else. Be who you are and remember that to be a Christian is more than just making that statement; it is showing up to service, paying your offering, preaching a good message, or even wearing a suit. It is putting on the whole armor of God and building your treasure in heaven, while passing through this earth as an example of a mirror of Christ.

And You Call Yourself a Christian by Darick Spears

It is running the full race and giving it 100%. It is loving God and your neighbor as yourself. It is forgiveness, not judging, speaking the truth, examining yourself daily, being brave and faithful to the end; all while being yourself.

Peace and Love.

www.ingramcontent.com/pod-product-compliance
Lightning Source LLC
Chambersburg PA
CBHW021003230426
43666CB00005B/259